BURNT STONE

A Testimony of
the Healing and Delivering Power of God

Zechariah 3 & 4
… is this not a brand plucked from the fire …

Virginia Douglas (Howe)

Burnt Stone: A Testimony of the Healing and Delivering Power of God

All emphasis within Scripture quotations is the author's own.

Please note that the publishing style used in this book does not always adhere to normal grammatical rules. Certain pronouns relating to the Father, Son and Holy Spirit are intentionally capitalised and in most cases the names relating to satan are not.

ISBN: 978-178456-302-8

A catalogue record for this book is available from the British Library.

First published 2016 by Fast-Print Publishing of Peterborough, England.

This book is written to encourage new believers to stand strong in their faith and in the Lord Jesus Christ.

Ephesians 6:10 says:

Finally, my brethren, be strong in the Lord,
and in the power of His might.

Dedication

Firstly, I would like to dedicate this book to the Holy Spirit who prompted me to write it and helped me to complete it.

I would also like to dedicate this book to my loving daughter Verona, my son Clive, my three grandsons Darren, Andre and Mark and my granddaughter Lawshon. But I would especially like to dedicate it to Verona and Darren, who after reading the first half of the book with much excitement, encouragement, hugs and kisses said, "I am proud of you mum" and "My gran is a writer!". May the God of heaven bless and keep them.

Acknowledgements

Firstly, I would like to acknowledge and thank the Lord Jesus who has helped me to write this book, something that I thought would be impossible for me to do. The Lord used six special women of God to encourage me, pray with me and help me in whatever way they could and I thank them for their love and prayers.

Two of those women are Elder Enid who is one of my current leaders and Deaconess Stephanie who is my former leader. Another is dear Minister Denise who is the editor of this book. As well as helping me to put this book together and find ways to make the book a success, she is also my tutor, sister in the Lord and a good friend. Then there is dear Sister Angela, a friend in need and a friend indeed who helped me through a difficult time of sickness, just as my own daughter would if she were not so far away in the U.S. When she read the book she was very excited and give me much encouragement.

There is also Sister Avril who took the time to read and correct my first manuscript and encourage me. Then there is Dr Pricilla, the one who God used to lead me to Christ many years ago as my spiritual mother, who continually prayed for me and gave me her overwhelming love and support. I am thankful to God for what He has done in my life. I praise GOD!

Many thanks to these six people who God has sent to help me. May the good Lord bless and keep them all. Amen!

Contents

Foreword

This book provides the path that will enable you to reflect on those moments in your life when no one else could have stepped in on your behalf but God. Although important and valuable, human effort would not have brought the level of intervention that one would have required in those moments.

Elder Virginia has brought home in a humorous and light-hearted manner, the harsh realities of her life's journey to this present day and how God in His infinite mercy made Himself known to her.

Elder Virginia's experiences represent the plight of one of our 'generals' in the Kingdom, who recognises that it would be unwise to withhold such significant episodes in her life, when they could make the world of difference to the lives of others; whether they are just beginning their life journey or right in the midst of it with its peaks and troughs. Moreover, whenever God did good things for the Jewish people, He always told them not to "*... hide them from their children, but tell to the coming generation the glorious deeds of the Lord, and his might, and the wonders that he has done.*" (Psalm 78:4 - ESV). He says, "*Let this be recorded for a generation to come, so that a people yet to be created may praise the Lord*" (Psalm 102:18 - ESV).

Therefore, if we truly regard ourselves as those Jews who were 'grafted in' (see Romans 11:17), then a life story like this should be highly regarded and valued, as well as warmly applauded.

Elder Yvonne Carr
Ruach City Church

Introduction

When I wrote this book I did not know what the title would be, but near the time of completion I asked the Lord, “What shall I call this book?” and I clearly heard in my spirit '*Burnt Stone*'. I asked “Why *Burnt Stone*?” and the Lord showed me a picture of a house made of stone but the house was on fire. He said that if I cleaned the stones they would be hard because they had been through fire. Bless God!

That got me thinking of all the things that I had been through and how each time I came out a little bruised but stronger than before. At times my work colleagues would ask “How is it that you went through all that … and you're still smiling?”, I told them, “It is the Lord!”.

Confirmation

About a week after the book was completed we had a live recording event at my church, which was on the 25th of April in that year to be exact. A visiting pastor from Wales was asked to speak and ... well, I almost fell off my seat when he began to talk about burnt stone! He even started to pray for people whom he called burnt stones because of what they had been through. I could hardly contain myself, I wanted to run and scream but I could not because of the live programme.

Then on the Sunday of that week, the co-pastor of my church preached a message from the passage of Scripture where God came down and confounded the language of the people at the Tower of Babel (see Genesis 11:1-9). On the Monday morning following the service I started to read Genesis chapter 11 and when I got to verse 3, I took a deep breath and read it again:

> *And they said one to another, go to, let us make brick and burn them thoroughly. And they had brick for 'stone'* ... (Genesis 11:3).

I was at home when I read it so I could shout and shout! I praised God for His confirmation. Praise be to God, look at God!

Part One: Burnt Stone

Chapter One

In the Beginning

My Inspiration

I was inspired by the Holy Spirit in July 1999 to write after attending Bible School for one year. At that time the Spirit of God was working in me mightily, so I thought I would write something about the Holy Spirit.

I began by reading Genesis chapter one, the book of beginnings. It reads:

> *In the beginning God created the heavens and the earth. The earth was without form, and void; and darkness was on the face of the deep. And the Spirit of God was hovering over the face of the waters* (Genesis 1:1-2).

This explained to me that the Holy Spirit is God. The Bible says: "*In the beginning was the Word, and the Word was with God, and the Word was God*" (John 1:1).

Creation and Restoration

Genesis 1:27-28 says that God created man in His own image and that in the image of God He created him, male and female. It goes on to say that God blessed them and told them to be fruitful, multiply, subdue the earth and have dominion. So then, if this was God's original intention for man, something must have happened to cause God to have to restore us. I believe that when man sinned, God had to restore us back to our original state because according to Genesis 1:31, everything God originally made was 'good'.

In Revelation 21:5 the Bible says, "*Behold, I make all things new*". The Bible also says:

> *Therefore, if anyone is in Christ, he is a new creation; old things have passed away; behold, all things have become new. Now all things are of God, who has reconciled us to Himself through Jesus Christ, and has given us the ministry of reconciliation* (2 Corinthians 5:17-18).

The 'Supposed' Reason

So what went wrong? The book of Revelation provides us with some insight. Chapter 12 says:

> *Now a great sign appeared in heaven: a woman clothed with the sun, with the moon under her feet, and on her head a garland of twelve stars* (Revelation 12:1).

> *And another sign appeared in heaven: behold, a great, fiery red dragon having seven heads and ten horns, and seven diadems on his heads* (Revelation 12:3).

The reason becomes clearer as the Scripture goes on to say:

> *And war broke out in heaven: Michael and his angels fought with the dragon; and the dragon and his angels fought, but they did not prevail, nor was a place found for them in heaven any longer* (Revelation 12:7-8).

> *Then I heard a loud voice saying in heaven, "Now salvation, and strength, and the kingdom of our God, and the power of His Christ have come, for the accuser of our brethren, who accused them before our God day and night, has been cast down"* (Revelation 12:10).

Satan was behind the war in heaven and he was the one who interrupted the original order of God's creation.

Satan

Satan is referred to in scripture as the 'devil', the 'great dragon', the 'old serpent' and 'Lucifer, son of the morning'. Praise God, scripture also tells us that we overcome him by the blood of the Lamb and by the word of our testimony. Through the cross, satan is defeated (see Philippians 2:1-11).

The book of Isaiah makes the following statement about satan:

> *How you are fallen from heaven, O Lucifer, son of the morning! How you are cut down to the ground, You who weakened the nations* (Isaiah 14:12).

God

God is a Spirit. The Bible tells us in John 4:24 that, "*God is Spirit, and those who worship Him must worship in spirit and truth*". God is also triune, which means that He consists of three distinct persons in one:

- The Father (*God*)
- The Son (*Jesus*)
- The Holy Spirit (*Spirit*)

Man

Man is also a triune being, consisting of three distinct parts:

- We are *Spirit*
- We have a *Soul*
- And we live in a *Body*

Man is triune because we are made in the image and likeness of God, which we see in the book of Genesis:

> *"Let Us make man in Our image, according to Our likeness ..."* (Genesis 1:26).

Hence we are first spirit, with a soul and both are housed in a body.

Chapter Two

An Introduction to the Holy Spirit

Who is the Holy Spirit?

The Bible gives us much insight into the characteristics of the Holy Spirit. We are told that He is the 'Spirit of truth' and that He is the 'Spirit of God', but Scripture also tells us that He is a person and that He speaks. The book of John says:

> *However, when He, the Spirit of truth, has come, He will guide you into all truth; for He will not speak on His own authority, but whatever He hears He will speak; and He will tell you things to come.* (John 16:13).

The Bible goes on to tell us even more about the nature of the Holy Spirit.

He can be grieved

Scripture tells us that it is possible for us to grieve the Holy Spirit:

> *And do not grieve the Holy Spirit of God, by whom you were sealed for the day of redemption* (Ephesians 4:30).

He is our Teacher and Comforter

The Holy Spirit is God in action. He is our teacher and our comforter:

> *But the Helper, the Holy Spirit, whom the Father will send in My name, He will teach you all things, and bring to your remembrance all things that I said to you* (John 14:26).

The book of Acts also shows Him as a comforter to the churches who were "… *walking in the fear of the Lord and in the comfort of the Holy Spirit …*" (Acts 9:31).

He is our Helper

The Apostle Paul wrote about the Holy Spirit as our helper in the book of Romans, making it clear that we need His help:

> *Likewise the Spirit also helps in our weaknesses. For we do not know what we should pray for as we ought, but the Spirit Himself makes intercession for us with groanings which cannot be uttered* (Romans 8:26).

Jesus also warned that it is important to reverence the Holy Spirit and that there are consequences for speaking against Him and for failing to acknowledge His works:

> *Anyone who speaks a word against the Son of Man, it will be forgiven him; but whoever speaks against*

> *the Holy Spirit, it will not be forgiven him, either in this age or in the age to come* (Matthew 12:32).

Before I became a born-again believer, I used to rely on an alarm clock to wake me up in the mornings, but when I became born-again in 1989, I began to ask the Holy Spirit to wake me up. Since then I have never used an alarm clock, why? Because I acknowledge the Holy Spirit as my helper and as the one who wakes me up every day without fail!

He is indeed our helper as stated in Romans 8:26.

The Personality of the Holy Spirit

Once we acknowledge the Holy Spirit as a person, we can begin to understand His nature and His many qualities. The Bible gives us great insight into the personality of the Holy Spirit.

He is not an experience

- He is not *a force*
- He is not *energy*
- He is not *just a power*
- He is not *an influence*
- He is *a person*

He is God in action

- *"He will teach you all things ..."* (John 14:26)
- *"He will testify of Me [Jesus] ..."* (John 15:26)
- *"He will guide you into all truth ..."* (John 16:13)
- *"He will glorify Me [Jesus] ..."* (John 16:14)

He has a mind

- He knows all things (see 1 Corinthians 2:10-11 and Acts 15:28)

He has emotions

- He feels and can be grieved (see Ephesians 4:30)

He has a will and He can choose

- He has a will which is in unity with the Father (see 1 Corinthians 12:11)

He speaks

- He speaks and instructs, but He will not say anything that is contrary to the Word of God (see Acts 13:2 and Acts 1:16)

He comforts and convicts

- He comforts and He also convicts us before leading us to repentance. Without conviction and repentance there is no change (see Acts 9:31 and Job 40-42)

The Character of the Holy Spirit

The Holy Spirit is 'omniscient'. This is an attribute by which God perfectly and eternally knows all things; past, present and future (see Psalm 147:5, Isaiah 46:10 and Proverbs 15:11).

He is 'omnipotent'. This is an attribute which describes His ability to do whatever He wills (see Job 42:2, Jeremiah 32:17 and Matthew 19:26).

He is 'omnipresent'. This is an attribute which describes how He fills the universe in all its parts. He is present everywhere all at once (see Psalm 139:7-12, Jeremiah 23:23-24 and Acts 17:27-28).

The Holy Spirit is God

The Holy Spirit is God. Genesis 3:8-9 indicates that He walked through the garden of Eden in the cool of the day, because when Adam and his wife heard the voice of the Lord, they "*... hid themselves from the presence of the Lord God ...*". When is the cool of the day? This is whenever God shows up, the Holy Spirit is the presence of God.

The Three are One

Jesus identified with God and the Bible tells us that they are equal:

> *Who, being in the form of God, did not consider it robbery to be equal with God* (Philippians 2:6).

This is also shown in John 5:18 where the Jews sought to kill Jesus because He made Himself equal with God. Further Scriptures which show the Father, Son and Holy Spirit as equal include:

> *Go therefore and make disciples of all the nations, baptizing them in the name of the Father and of the Son and of the Holy Spirit* (Matthew 28:19).

The grace of the Lord Jesus Christ, and the love of God, and the communion of the Holy Spirit be with you all (2 Corinthians 13:14).

For there are three that bear witness in heaven: the Father, the Word, and the Holy Spirit; and these three are one (1 John 5:7).

Chapter Three

The Baptism and Anointing of the Holy Spirit

The Power of the Holy Spirit

It was the Holy Spirit that showed up at Pentecost in the Bible when the disciples received power from on high and spoke in the language of other nations (see Acts 2:1-4).

The power of the Holy Spirit is also seen in Luke 1:28-35, when the angel Gabriel was sent by God to announce the birth of Christ to Mary. It was by the power of the Holy Spirit that Christ was conceived:

> *And the angel answered and said to her, "The Holy Spirit will come upon you, and the power of the Highest will overshadow you; therefore, also, that Holy One who is to be born will be called the Son of God …"* (Luke 1:35).

The Baptism of the Holy Spirit

The baptism of the Holy Spirit is a complete immersion into the Spirit of God, through the Holy Spirit. This is what the one hundred and twenty disciples were instructed to wait for in Acts 1:1-4 and what they then received in Acts 2:1-4. The Bible tells us that they were gathered in one place and in one accord, in unity and in prayer when God sent His Holy Spirit upon them, as like fire.

The Holy Spirit is represented by fire, wind, water, breath, oil and Spirit (Ruach). He can be like a rushing mighty wind, or a still small voice and 1 Kings 19 illustrates this:

> *And a great and strong wind tore into the mountains and broke the rocks in pieces before the Lord, but the Lord was not in the wind; and after the wind an earthquake, but the Lord was not in the earthquake; and after the earthquake a fire, but the Lord was not in the fire; and after the fire a still small voice* (1 Kings 19:11-12).

Romans 5:5 tells us that it is by the Holy Spirit that the love of God dwells in us, "... *because the love of God has been poured out in our hearts by the Holy Spirit who was given to us*". The Holy Spirit is referred to as the 'Holy Ghost' in some translations of the Bible, but they are one and the same. Both titles refer to the Spirit of the Lord.

The Holy Spirit Anoints

It is the Holy Spirit who anoints us to become ministers of the gospel. In the book of Luke, Jesus quoted this from the book of Isaiah:

> *The Spirit of the Lord is upon Me, Because He has anointed Me to preach the gospel to the poor ...* (Luke 4:18).

The anointing of the Holy Spirit was also evident when Jesus was baptised. The Bible tells us that heaven opened and the Holy Spirit descended upon Him. This is the moment when Jesus was anointed for His ministry (see Luke 3:21-23 and John 1:32-33).

Scripture also shows us how Jesus was 'led' by the Holy Spirit:

> *Then Jesus, being filled with the Holy Spirit, returned from the Jordan and was led by the Spirit into the wilderness* (Luke 4:1).

The Holy Spirit Quickens

The Holy Spirit 'quickens' us, which means that He makes us come alive. We see in the Bible that the first man Adam was made a 'living soul', then Jesus, who is referred to as the last Adam was made a 'quickening Spirit' (see 1 Corinthians 15:45). The book of Romans speaks about the quickening of the Holy Spirit in this way:

> *But if the Spirit of Him who raised Jesus from the dead dwells in you, He who raised Christ from the dead will also give life to your mortal bodies through His Spirit who dwells in you* (Romans 8:11).

We Need the Holy Spirit

The Holy Spirit dwells in us when we become born again and we become sons and daughters of the living God:

> *And because you are sons, God has sent forth the Spirit of His Son into your hearts, crying out, "Abba, Father!"* (Galatians 4:6).

As Christians we must have the anointing of the Holy Spirit in our lives. Our Christian walk must be in spirit and in truth, why? Because "*God is a Spirit, and they that worship Him, must worship Him in spirit and truth*" (John 4:24). We cannot make it on our own. It is the Holy Spirit that gives us the power to do the will of God. As we can see from the portrayal of Jesus' baptism in Luke 3:22-23, even Jesus Himself needed the help of the Holy Spirit.

So then, if we want to have this anointing in our lives, we must go back to the message of the cross and surrender our lives completely to Jesus. This is the secret of the anointing! We must surrender all to Jesus, then take up the cross and follow Him. In other words, we must die to self. Jesus said:

> *Unless a grain of wheat falls into the ground and dies, it remains alone; but if it dies, it produces much grain* (John 12:24).

Therefore even in our suffering, we must depend totally on Him (see Philippians 2:5-9).

God Reveals by His Spirit

God reveals the hidden things to us by His Spirit:

> *But as it is written: "Eye has not seen, nor ear heard, nor have entered into the heart of man the things which God has prepared for those who love Him". But God has revealed them to us through His Spirit* (1 Corinthians 2:9-10).

> *Surely the Lord God does nothing, unless He reveals His secret to His servants the prophets* (Amos 3:7).

This tells us that when God is pleased with us, He sends His Spirit and reveals to us what He has prepared and what is in His heart towards us.

One of the Three

The Holy Spirit is the third person of the Godhead, which includes the Father, the Son and the Holy Spirit. He is our chief executive here on earth, He is power, He is fire, He is the anointing that breaks every yoke and He anoints us with power and might ... He is God! The book of Zechariah says:

> *'Not by might nor by power, but by My Spirit,'*
> *Says the Lord of hosts* (Zechariah 4:6).

He is Wonderful

The Holy Spirit is the most wonderful person in the world! It is important that we get to know Him. Not only does He live within us, He also walks with us, but when it comes to knowing the personality of the Holy Spirit, this has to be revealed to us:

> *But God has revealed them to us through His Spirit. For the Spirit searches all things, yes, the deep things of God* (1 Corinthians 2:10).

God created us in His own image, so that He can express Himself through us by His Spirit, because God is a Spirit.

Important!

Children of God, it is very important that we do not speak against the Holy Spirit, we must be careful of our words. The Bible warns us to be careful about what we speak:

> *Do not be rash with your mouth, And let not your heart utter anything hastily before God ...* *(*Ecclesiastes 5:2).

When we give our heart to the Lord, He puts His Spirit within us which brings our human spirit to life, so we must give due reverence to the Holy Spirit, which is the Spirit of the Lord.

Chapter Four

The Work of the Holy Spirit

The Manifestation of God Through the Holy Spirit

The reason I am writing about the Holy Spirit and talking about God and Jesus is because we need to understand that the three are one. The Bible tells us:

> *For there are three that bear witness in heaven: the Father, the Word, and the Holy Spirit; and these three are one* (1 John 5:7).

Jesus Himself said that He does nothing independently of God the Father:

> *The Son can do nothing of Himself, but what He sees the Father do; for whatever He does, the Son also does in like manner* (John 5:19).

As believers, we must seek the power of the Holy Spirit and know that it comes from God. The Holy Spirit is the manifestation of the power of God. When we receive the Holy Spirit, we will not move according to what we see but by the power of God. The Apostle Paul wrote:

> *For I am not ashamed of the gospel of Christ, for it is the power of God to salvation ...* (Romans 1:16).

The Baptism of the Holy Spirit

When we receive the baptism of the Holy Spirit, we are filled with the power of God. The baptism of the Holy Spirit is for every person who believes in their heart and confesses with their mouth that Jesus Christ has risen from the dead. We need this experience to enable us to preach the gospel of Jesus Christ with power.

Before sending His disciples to preach the gospel, Jesus breathed on them and told them "*Receive the Holy Spirit*" (John 20:22). He told them:

> *But you shall receive power when the Holy Spirit has come upon you; and you shall be witnesses to Me in Jerusalem, and in all Judea and Samaria, and to the end of the earth* (Acts 1:8).

As discussed in the previous chapter, the Bible tells us that the disciples were filled with the Holy Spirit at Pentecost (Acts 2:1-4).

Baptism in Water

The work of the Holy Spirit is not only evident when we receive the baptism of the Holy Spirit, but also when we are baptised in water (see Matthew 3:11). The word baptism (baptise) is symbolic of washing or cleansing and the very first time God commanded washing to take place in Scripture was in the Mosaic Law (see Exodus 30:17-

21). Baptism in water (being fully immersed in water) is connected with repentance and Christian baptism symbolises a union with Christ:

> *For as many of you as were baptized into Christ have put on Christ* (Galatians 3:27).

When we ask Jesus to come into our hearts and accept Him as our Lord and Saviour, the next step is to be baptised in water. Mark 16:16 says, "*He who believes and is baptized will be saved ...*". The purpose of being baptised in water is for the remission (removing) of our sins. The Bible says:

> *Repent, and let every one of you be baptized in the name of Jesus Christ for the remission of sins; and you shall receive the gift of the Holy Spirit* (Acts 2:38).

Water baptism allows us to identify with Christ in His death, burial and resurrection (see Romans 6:3-5) and we receive the blessings of baptism by faith (see Galatians 3:26). The Bible tells us:

> *Do you not know that as many of us as were baptized into Christ Jesus were baptized into His death* (Romans 6:3).

> *But if the Spirit of Him who raised Jesus from the dead dwells in you, He who raised Christ from the dead will also give life to your mortal bodies through His Spirit who dwells in you* (Romans 8:11).

The Anointing

The Bible tells us that Jesus is the 'anointed one' and that the anointing is the power of God (see Acts 10:37-38). The anointing of the Holy Spirit beautifies us, it preserves us and it empowers us to fulfil the call of God on our lives. The work of the Holy Spirit through the anointing, is also a manifestation of the Shekinah glory of God - which is the presence of God.

The book of Isaiah tells us that the anointing is the burden removing, yoke destroying power of God:

> *It shall come to pass in that day That his burden will be taken away from your shoulder, And his yoke from your neck, And the yoke will be destroyed because of the anointing oil* (Isaiah 10:27).

God gives the following warning about His anointing in the book of Psalms:

> *Do not touch My anointed ones, And do My prophets no harm* (Psalm 105:15).

The Umpire

The Holy Spirit is the umpire of our soul, He can disqualify us when we are in the wrong, but He always deals with us fairly. He will always warn us when we are about to do wrong, but we will only be in trouble if we do not listen.

Even though the Holy Spirit lives within us, when we grieve Him by sinning, for example when we continually lie, He will eventually depart from us because He is the Spirit of truth. The Bible says:

> *My Spirit shall not strive with man forever, for he is indeed flesh ...* (Genesis 6:3).

Sometimes people ask "Why do we have to invite the Holy Spirit into our heart?". The Bible helps us to understand this when it tells us that the heart of a man is desperately wicked (see Jeremiah 17:9). When David sinned, he prayed the following prayer which is found in the book of Psalms:

> *Create in me a clean heart, O God, And renew a steadfast spirit within me. Do not cast me away from Your presence, And do not take Your Holy Spirit from me* (Psalm 51:10-11).

So from this we can see why we need to repent of our sins, seek forgiveness and invite the Holy Spirit into our heart.

The story of Ananias and his wife Sapphira is a prime example of what could happen when we lie to the Holy Spirit (see Acts 5:1-11). Even a small lie can grieve the Holy Spirit. Thanks be to God that we are now living in the dispensation of His grace, however we should not take the Holy Spirit for granted. He is the Spirit of truth!

The Promise of God

When God redeemed us He also adopted us into His Kingdom as sons and daughters:

> *Because you are sons, God has sent forth the Spirit of His Son into your hearts, crying out, "Abba, Father!"* (Galatians 4:6).

> *For as many as are led by the Spirit of God, these are sons of God* (Romans 8:14).

> *The Spirit Himself bears witness with our spirit that we are children of God* (Romans 8:16).

God made this promise to us in the book of Joel:

> *And it shall come to pass afterward that I will pour out My Spirit on all flesh; Your sons and your daughters shall prophesy, Your old men shall dream dreams, Your young men shall see visions* (Joel 2:28).

Acts 2:17-18 also speaks of this promise.

It is a wonderful thing for us to have the fire of the Holy Spirit burning in our hearts. How can we live without His presence? God has given us His Spirit of wisdom, knowledge and understanding so that we may know Him and the power of His resurrection.

Witnesses

The reason Jesus (God) gave us the Holy Spirit is so that we can be His witnesses:

> *But you shall receive power when the Holy Spirit has come upon you; and you shall be witnesses to*

> *Me in Jerusalem, and in all Judea and Samaria, and to the end of the earth* (Acts 1:8).

> *No one can say that Jesus is Lord except by the Holy Spirit* (1 Corinthians 12:3).

Just as the disciples were in one accord, in unity and in one place in the upper room waiting to receive the Holy Ghost, we too must be in unity and receive the promise of God. (see Acts 1:4).

Because the Holy Spirit lives in us, He preserves us physically and spiritually and we are renewed like an eagle, (see Psalm 103:5). Just think how privileged we are to have the Spirit of God dwelling inside of us and working with us in the things of God. Truly God loves us with an everlasting love.

The Spirit at Work

In Scripture, the Spirit of the Lord came upon Samson mightily and he killed a young kid (goat) with his bare hands and slew a thousand men with the jawbone of an ass (see Judges 14:6 and 15:15-16). Sometimes we forget who we have living on the inside of us.

In 1 John 4:4, the Bible tells us that He who is in us is greater than he who is in the world. As we can see from the example of Samson, when the Holy Spirit comes upon the people of God they do mighty things. It is the Holy Spirit that gives believers the courage and wisdom to become leaders.

He will prompt us to do things that we have never done before but He does not force us, so we have to be sensitive otherwise we could miss it. Jesus moves in countless ways, but He is very specific in His timing and His activities. In Scripture, His actions were always according to what the Father told Him to do.

The Holy Spirit can also be imparted upon us by the Lord in a similar way to when God told Moses to gather seventy men, He imparted his spirit upon them so that they could minister to others effectively (see Numbers 11:17). The Holy Spirit imparts the things of God into our hearts, such as godly desire for example.

The Holy Spirit is the 'breath of God', so He is a creative force. In the book of Genesis we read that God made man out of clay, from the dust of the ground. He breathed into him the breath of life and man became a living soul (see Genesis 2:7), but God gives us a spirit when He breathes into us and our spirit bears witness with His Spirit. When we are baptised by His Spirit, we are filled with the Holy Spirit. We are filled with the breath of God.

The Holy Spirit also determines the spiritual gifts and skills that we receive. He alone distributes these gifts and decides which gifts each person should have. The Bible says:

> *There are diversities of gifts, but the same Spirit* (1 Corinthians 12:4).

Jesus had to return to His father in order for the Holy Spirit to be given to us. Jesus said:

> *It is to your advantage that I go away; for if I do not go away, the Helper will not come to you; but if I depart, I will send Him to you* (John 16:7).

Jesus also talks about this in John 15:26.

It is important that we are in communication with the Holy Spirit, since He reveals Jesus and the Father to us and because He is our helper. He is the Spirit of truth and He will guide us into all truth. We cannot do without Him and even Jesus needed Him.

Gifts of the Holy Spirit

The Holy Spirit gave us gifts, nine to be exact and these gifts are listed in 1 Corinthians 12:1-11. The nine gifts are as follows:

- *Word of Wisdom* (1 Kings 3:16-28; John 8:3-7)
- *Word of Knowledge* (John 4:16-19; Acts 5: 1-10)
- *Gift of Faith* (Romans 10:17)
- *Gifts of Healing* (Mark 16:18)
- *Working of Miracles* (Matthew 9:2-8)
- *Gift of Prophecy* (1 Corinthians 14:3, 31-39)
- *Gift of Discernment* (Acts 16:16-18)
- *Gift of Different Tongues* (1 Corinthians 14:5, 27)
- *Interpretation of Tongues* (1 Corinthians 14:13)

Empowerment

We need the empowerment of the Holy Spirit in order to be effective (see Acts 1:8). Jesus Himself was empowered by the Holy Spirit before starting His ministry:

> *And John bore witness, saying, "I saw the Spirit descending from heaven like a dove, and He remained upon Him"* (John 1:32).

Jesus told His disciples to wait for the Holy Spirit who would empower them for service:

> *Behold, I send the Promise of My Father upon you; but tarry in the city of Jerusalem until you are endued with power from on high* (Luke 24:49).

> *And they were all filled with the Holy Spirit and began to speak with other tongues, as the Spirit gave them utterance* (Acts 2:4).

That is why the baptism of the Holy Spirit is a must, we cannot do without His power.

Chapter Five

The Healing Power of God: My Personal Testimonies

God Heals Today, Praise God!

I pray that my personal testimonies will bless somebody who may be going through the same things that I have been through. The Bible declares to us in Revelation 12:11, that we overcome him (satan) by the blood of the Lamb and by the word of our testimony.

The Gate

Before I tell you about my healing, let me share this with you. I am one of those people who God speaks to in dreams and visions and shortly before I became sick the first time, I saw an elderly man come into my room in a dream.

He told me that he wanted to show me something then he took me by the hand and led me through a large iron gate. We walked through the gate into a meadow and I have never seen such splendour and beauty. I looked up at him and said, "This is beautiful ..." and he responded, "Yes it is". We continued to walk and it was as though we were going up a hill. For a moment I stopped and looked over my shoulder to see that beautiful meadow again. Throughout this time the man said nothing.

We continued to walk up the hill then we went through a cloud, it was so beautiful and heavenly. I looked up at him with excitement and he just smiled with approval as though he was happy for me. I have never seen such beauty, it felt like heaven to me. If I may boldly say so ... it was heaven indeed!

Voices

Then I heard voices singing. It sounded like thousands of voices singing in one accord and it was so melodious and harmonious, so sweet ... it's hard to explain. I listened intently while the man just kept looking down at me and smiling. We stayed there for a while, then he said to me "It's time to go back", but I would not have it. I told him no I wanted to stay, but he said that I have to go back because my family needed me.

I was so upset (rebellion in heaven)! Well, he just held my hand and we walked back down the hill through the beautiful meadow and back through the large black gate, then he said goodbye to me. I stood for a while and watched him go. He looked back at me and bowed his head as if to say, "It's all right", then I started to walk back towards my house. When I awoke I found that I was still in my bed.

I could not go back to sleep, I just laid there meditating on the heavenly vision I had just had. It was not long after this that I became sick, but praise be to God, His word came to me saying, "You shall not die, but you shall live to declare the works of the Lord", (see Psalm 118:17).

My Testimony (1)

Healed by the Power of God

In the summer of 1993 I had a major operation that caused me to be out of work for three months. The operation took place at the hospital where I work and the team of doctors and nurses were baffled by my recovery.

Within two days I was up and out of bed and they said that they had never seen anyone recover from this kind of operation so quickly. Why was that? Because my God had started the healing process! I went home after just one week, whereas others who had gone through the same operation took three weeks or more to recover. That was God's power at work in me, praise Him!

At Home

When I returned home, I was only able to walk slowly and I was a little bent over as a result of the operation, but I could still do my housework. Then one night I went to bed and had another dream. I saw someone come into my room and I knew it was the Lord.

He sat on my bed, put his arm around me and said, "I am going to heal you now". He then picked me up in his arms and rocked me back and forth like a baby, before putting me back to bed and saying, "It is all right now". The next morning when I woke up, I felt totally healed within myself and started to walk upright and much more quickly. I had no words to explain how I felt, God proved to me that He is a healer and that nothing was too hard for Him.

I know that I am important to God because He healed me according to His word:

> *He was wounded for our transgressions, He was bruised for our iniquities; The chastisement for our peace was upon Him, And by His stripes we are healed* (Isaiah 53:5).

> *Who Himself bore our sins in His own body on the tree, that we, having died to sins, might live for righteousness: by whose stripes you were healed* (1 Peter 2:24).

I am a witness that Jesus still heals today. To God be the glory!

My Testimony (2)

Another Healing

In June 1997, God healed my broken body again. I was struck down with an illness which goes by the medical name of Labyrinthitis. Let me try to describe this illness. It is a condition where there is a total loss of balance and where the fluid in the ear canal becomes infected, causing a person to constantly lose their balance. It is as though the whole world is spinning at a hundred miles an hour and you lose the use of every limb in your body.

Even when I would lay on the floor, I could hardly move. It was like I was on a spinning wheel. I felt like my head was coming off my body and my body felt like it was coming apart. I could not speak properly, my speech was slurred and I truly thought that I was going to die.

What Happened Next

The illness came on slowly over a period of two weeks, then one morning as I awoke, before opening my eyes I felt like someone was spinning my bed around. I was very scared but managed to get out of the bed, with much difficulty.

I dragged myself on my belly into my front room. With great difficulty I then picked up the phone and dialled my son's number, I was not even sure that anyone would be home because my son and his girlfriend usually left for work early. Don't ask me why I called their number, but I did and for some reason my son's girlfriend was still at home and answered the phone. She told me that she was late leaving the house that day, but I knew that my Lord had kept her at home for this purpose.

My Speech

My speech was not clear and all I could say was "Sick … am sick …", because by this point I could not move. She said she would call an ambulance. I managed to call my workplace and one of the nurses answered, so I said to her "Am sick … can't move …". The nurse asked me a few questions but I could not answer her, then I heard her saying, "Get the ambulance, it's Virg". With that, I turned slowly to make my way to the front door still on my belly, which took me a while. As I got closer to the front door, I wondered how on earth I was going to open it.

I began to slowly pull myself up by leaning on my hands and I tried to get into a kneeling position. After trying for a while, with a great deal of difficulty but with the help of the Lord I managed to pull myself up and open the front door. In my distress I called out to God "Help me!". I remembered Psalm 18:6 which says, "*In my distress I called upon the Lord, And cried out to my God; He heard my voice from His temple ...*".

By this time the ambulance, the police and my son's girlfriend all arrived at the same time, in fact two ambulances came in the end. I could not reach the intercom button to let them in, but thankfully a neighbour must have let them in, praise God!

The first thing the police officer said was "It must be drugs". I was laying across the front door as I could not move and I was trying to tell them it was not drugs, but the police officer continued asking me how much I had taken. My speech came back a little, so I told them "I do not take drugs, I am just sick".

Hospital Number One

The paramedics came in and took me to hospital. The doctors did not seem to know what the problem was, so they did some tests. They were still unsure so they sent me to see a consultant who seemed to be an expert.

The consultant requested more tests but still could not find the reason for the illness, so they eventually diagnosed it as Labyrinthitis because it had happened before. The next day I asked to be transferred to the hospital where I worked and at that precise moment, a nurse came in and said that my nursing officer from work was on the phone asking them to transfer me to that hospital!

Hospital Number Two

When the ambulance arrived at the hospital where I worked, it was as though royalty had arrived … well I am a child of the King, Jesus! Most of the staff were waiting for me with tears in their eyes and I felt so loved, it had to be God.

When they took me to my room I was stunned. There were flowers and cards everywhere! I know that it was God. I was very popular and if I might say so, a very good worker who is known as a woman of God because I never hide who Jesus is. People respected me for who I am and some even called me 'Father Virg' jokingly, praise God!

There were still some colleagues who could not stand me because of the Jesus in me and I was not afraid to expose them for who they were, bless God, but wait for this ... these were the very same people who had dressed up my room using their own money, look at God! He said in His word that He will prepare a table before us in the presence of our enemies (Psalm 23:5).

Consultants were called to examine me. One of them was a neurologist who sent me to have an MRI brain scan. The scan showed that a blood vessel had burst on the left side of my brain, so they started treatment. At this time I still could not move by myself, but I was well cared for by the nursing staff, thanks be to God. My body began to respond slightly to the medication, but the doctors were still not happy so they sent me for more tests. Some even said that I might never walk again, but that's when God stepped in! Beloved friends, when man said no, God said yes!

My Miracle

On the night of the third day of the illness at about 3am, I had a vision/dream. I saw a very tall handsome man, maybe in his early forties ... God knows me very well (smile) who came into my room. He sat on the edge of my bed and picked me up in his arms as one would pick up a baby. He then said to me, "I am going to heal you now". He reached into his pocket and took out a small bottle of oil and asked me if I had a container. I pointed to a table beside the bed where a small bowl and some cotton-wool swabs were and he dipped a cotton-wool swab into the oil and began to bathe my inner ear. He did it so tenderly, just like a mother nursing her baby and I could feel the oil going around my head.

When he had finished he said to me "You will be fine now". With that, he said, "It's time to go". I asked him to stay but he just smiled and said, "You are healed now". Praise God! He then walked towards the door, but I was still begging him to stay. He stood at the door and looked back at me, nodding his head in agreement with what he had said to me (it is finished), then he smiled again and left.

After he left I woke up, got out of bed and went to the bathroom, pushing the drip stand with me as I walked. Friends, please bear in mind that previously I could not get out of bed on my own, it was the nurses who would take me to the bathroom. When I came back from the bathroom I sat on the bed and when I realised what I had just done I froze. I did not know whether to press the 'call' button or whether to scream. I could not even do that, so I just sat there saying, "Thank you Jesus, you healed me!". I could not go back to sleep, but thank God it was early morning so I got back into bed, sat up and waited for the first person to come into the room.

At about 5.30am a nurse came into the room, praise God that she was a Christian. I shouted out her name twice and said, "I am healed! God came into my room and healed me!". Another nurse came running into the room when she heard my shout, so I told them what had taken place earlier. The nurse that was a Christian was jumping and praising God, but the other nurse did not know what to do, so she ran from the room with tears in her eyes. Later when she came back into the room she looked at me with joy and said, "I can't believe what I am hearing!".

Later on that day, other staff came in to see me after hearing the report and they asked me about what had happened. They could not believe their eyes when they saw me sitting up in bed, so I told them that my God had healed me. Whether they believed it or not, the fact remains that the night before they had to bathe me and put me to bed, but that morning I had been able to get up and sit in a chair by myself.

What a mighty God we serve, bless His holy name! Friends, please understand, we serve a God that still heals today. He is the same yesterday, today and forever, He is

'Je-ho-vah Rapha' our healer and that is the reason why God sent His Son, Jesus. The Bible says:

> *But to you who fear My name The Sun of Righteousness shall arise With healing in His wings* (Malachi 4:2).

God tells us in His word that by the stripes of His Son Jesus we are healed:

> *But He was wounded for our transgressions, He was bruised for our iniquities; The chastisement for our peace was upon Him, And by His stripes we are healed* (Isaiah 53:5). Also see 1 Peter 2:24.

In Isaiah 43:2, the Bible also tells us that when we pass through the waters He will be with us and when we pass through the rivers, they will not overflow us and when we walk through the fire, we shall not be burned, neither shall the flames kindle upon us.

Beloved friends, God can use men and women (doctors) to fulfil His word. He gives them knowledge, wisdom and understanding in the area of medicine to help us. He also uses those who are called by His name. The Bible says:

> *They will lay hands on the sick, and they will recover* (Mark 16:18).

> *Is anyone among you sick? Let him call for the elders of the church, and let them pray over him,*

> *anointing him with oil in the name of the Lord. And the prayer of faith will save the sick, and the Lord will raise him up. And if he has committed sins, he will be forgiven* (James 5:14-15).

Praise God!

The Work of God

After I was healed, God began to use me in the same hospital where I worked and where I had also been a patient. I would go to work early in the mornings and pray all through the wards. I would also pray in the consulting rooms before the staff came in. I was one of the staff members who would bathe the patients in their beds, so I was able to pray while I worked. I never came across any sick person who said no to prayers, so I would just smile, pray and sing, I was known for my singing (bless God).

God showed Himself strong. People who I had prayed for were getting better and going home, but only God and the patients knew that I was praying. I had to be discreet because it was a private hospital, so the longer the patients stayed the better it was for the hospital as they would make more money. Eventually word got out that I was praying for the patients and many people were not happy, but that did not stop me from praying even more.

As time went on, I was led to pray more for people with cancer. The first patient I prayed for was a lady from Germany who was dying of cancer. I will never forget the morning when the staff in charge asked me to sit with this lady while she called her family. I began to feel a stirring in my spirit and I went into the room. The lady had already received surgery, so I held her hand and began to pray. I remember a man by the name of Hezekiah in 2 Kings 20:1-11 who was dying but called upon the Lord and God gave him fifteen more years to live, so I stood in the gap (interceded) for the lady.

The Results

When I began to pray I could feel the power of God flowing through me. As God would have it, her family took a long time to arrive, so I was hoping that the nurses would not come into the room as I continued to pray in tongues (in the Spirit).

The lady began to be sick and something began to ooze from her wound that did not smell good. I opened the window and cleaned her up while I continued to pray. Suddenly she held my hand and began to speak to me in her native German language, but obviously I could not understand her. I continued to pray (in tongues) and she smiled, as though she could understand what I was saying.

When the nurses and the doctor and her family members came in they were amazed. The lady started talking to her daughter and they were all looking at me. The daughter said something in German but I told her I didn't understand, so she then said it in English. She was thanking me for praying for her mother. After the doctors left the room, I asked the woman's daughter how she knew that I had prayed. She said her mother understood some of what I was saying and that they were

Christians. God must have allowed her to hear what I was saying, even though I myself did not know what I was saying as I was praying unto God in tongues.

Well, before the family left we exchanged phone numbers and kept in touch. Two weeks later, they took her to a hospice and she lived for another year before she died. What am I saying? She did not die when man said so, she died when God said so. This is just one example of God's handiwork and it was the beginning of my faith being strengthened.

In the end, the hospital found some excuse to move me from working on the ward to working in the outpatients department. They did not realise that prayer knows no boundaries!

Tongues

The Bible tells us that:

> *For he who speaks in a tongue does not speak to men but to God, for no one understands him; however, in the spirit he speaks mysteries* (1 Corinthians 14:2).

That is why I said that God must have allowed the woman to understand what I was saying when I was praying.

The Outpatients Department

Working in the outpatients department was another story! That's where I really began to see God's power at work. When staff were in trouble they would come to me for prayer. When their family needed help, even for things such as school placements, they would ask me to pray. That is what I was there for. God is no respecter of persons.

Doctors told one lady that she could not have children because of her bad back. I laid my hand on her back, then went home and stormed heaven (prayed) on her behalf. Bless the Lord, it was not long before she had two children ... praise God!

What the Lord showed me was that He was going to use me and that He was going to show me some things that were happening. There were staff members who came to work at the hospital who used other powers, but God would show them to me before they came. I would pray and they could not stay for long. I had to confront one person face-to-face. I told her that if she was willing to stop what she was doing and accept Jesus Christ as her saviour God would give her His power, but she refused. After a while I told her that one of us is going to leave but it would not be me, well she was the one who went! I called her 'mystic-meg'. Praise be to God!

There was another doctor at the hospital who specialised in hypnotising patients, but he did not stay long either. I would pray in his room and even though he was located in a quiet part of the hospital, he started to complain that it was too noisy. They moved him to another treatment room close to where I worked giving me easy access. I prayed every morning before the staff came in, then one day he could no longer stand it and he left. The great thing about it was that all the staff knew that I was praying. I did not hide what I was doing, bless the name of the Lord! Amen!

My Testimony (3)

In May 2001 I went to Jamaica for my mother's 80th birthday. It was a family reunion and I had not seen two of my sisters for many years due to them living in the USA. Well, this was a holiday to remember!

All the family had such a great time. We talked about our childhood, including all the good things that had happened as well as the bad things too. All in all, we had a wonderful time. We had so much fun, especially when mother tried to treat us like little girls. It was all so funny! Mother's children include four daughters and one son, just imagine how noisy we were. Mother begged us not to visit her all at once again! After two days with us she was fed up, but in a nice way of course, bless her heart!

After three wonderful weeks I came back to London. Within a week of me being back something strange happened. One night I went to bed and all was well. I woke up at about 3 a.m. feeling dizzy, with tingling in my hands and feet. I thought it was just cramps from the way that I was sleeping, but then my head started to hurt. After a while the tingling stopped so I got out of bed, but suddenly I could not remember where I was. After a while my memory came back, so I went to make a cup of tea.

As I picked up the cup, my hand fell lifelessly by my side and my feet gave way under me. It was a good thing that the cup was empty. I tried to pray but I could not speak and my memory went again. When I came to myself, I was laying on the floor. I attempted to pray but the words could not leave my mouth. To tell you the truth I was scared because I could not move and I could not talk.

It was frightening to say the least. In the morning, I did not want to stay on my own so I got ready and made my way to work. I felt dizzy on the bus and several times my bag fell without me knowing, but someone picked it up for me and with the help of God I managed get to work.

Passed Out

When I got to work I must have passed out again, because when I opened my eyes nurses and doctors were standing over me. They took me to an empty room and I could hear them asking me when the illness had started, but I could not speak well. My speech was slurred so they could not understand what I was saying. They checked my blood pressure and the reading was 185/200, very high indeed! From there they took me to a ward, put up a drip and gave me fluid and medication to bring my blood pressure down.

After that they took me for an x-ray. After the x-ray I was laying on the bed and I could see that the technicians were not happy, I could tell by the look on their faces. From there they took me to have an MRI brain scan. The scan showed that I had bleeding on my brain on both sides, so they called the neurologist, who started me on medication straight away.

The x-ray showed that the main large artery that carries the blood to my brain was blocked. It also showed that one of the smaller arteries was weak and my heart was enlarged, so they called a cardiologist. He did another test called an angiography where a small camera was put fed down into my chest with some dye on in while I slept. He diagnosed it as a stroke, or a 'transient ischemic attack' to use the correct term. My brain had been starved of its blood supply, hence the stroke, so the doctor then started me on medication, praise be to God!

Prior to this I had been on medication for high blood pressure for a few years, but after a while I had stopped taking it just to have a break. At times I would forget to have my blood pressure checked because I felt so well, but it seems that the excitement from my trip to Jamaica must have triggered it off. Anyway, I stayed in hospital for just over a week.

The Doctor's Report

One doctor said that I might have to be in a wheelchair, but I am glad he only said 'might' and I rejected his report! In Isaiah 53:1, the Bible talks about which report you choose to believe, well I chose to believe the report of the Lord which says that "... *with his stripes we are healed*" (Isaiah 53:5).

You see, God showed me my future. He showed me some of the things I would be doing and some of the places I would go, so there was no way He was going to keep me in a wheelchair because I was going to need my hands and feet to carry out these tasks. Praise Him! I believe that God was waiting to hear a negative report so He could step in and prove that He is God.

Standing on God's Promises

When man says no, God says yes! I stood on the promises of God and my healing began. The Lord said that He would heal me so I stood on the Word of God, including Psalm 103:1-5, Isaiah 53:1-5, 1 Peter 2:24 and particularly Malachi 4:2 "*But to you who fear My name The Sun of Righteousness shall arise With healing in His wings ...*".

Home

After I returned home the attacks continued and I will not lie, fear came over me every time but I stood on the Word of God and reminded myself that God has not given me a spirit of fear, however it was not easy. The worst part was when I wanted to speak and the words could not come out of my mouth, this was scary. It was funny at times, because someone would be speaking to me about something and I would give them a totally different response to what they were saying. Those who did not know about the illness looked at me as though I was crazy, wouldn't you?

A friend of mine who took me to church during that time (Miss A) was an absolute godsend. On our way to church she would talk to me about church and I would answer by talking about the hospital or work. She would look over at me and we would burst out laughing. Sometimes when she said something to me I would look at her as if she was mad. We would laugh all the way to church.

I am sure the enemy was mad! Sometimes in church I would stand up to praise God in worship and would fall flat on my face. The ushers would cover me because they thought that I fell under the power of God, but little did they know! However one thing I noticed is that when I fell, my body would feel like it was on fire and the power of God would be all over me. It was funny how no one tried to pick me up, I knew then that God was healing me every time.

I remember that one Sunday during worship, as I stood up with me hands raised and gave a loud shout I felt a strong breeze on my face and over I went, totally legless! My body was hot, but when I got up I felt strong. Praise God!

In church when the illness came over me, my Bible and writing pad would fall out of my hand, my speech would go and all I could do was look. Someone would pick them up for me but because I couldn't speak I would just smile at them. I could not even take notes because I would not remember a word the preacher said. At times I would begin to write the first word, then the book and pen would fall again and the rest is history. Very frustrating, but God!

When these things happened to me at work the nurses would put me in a room for a while or get someone to take me home. When I went home by bus I would sometimes go past my stop because I couldn't remember where to get off the bus. Sometimes I got to the end of the line where the bus driver would have to direct me to my home. What could I do but laugh, even though it was not funny. I had to see the funny side, especially when I would take the wrong bus, but praise God for His mercies!

One night at church I was jumping up and down and praising God because I was so excited that I could use my legs and wave my hands, God had healed me! I could talk and jump. I was sitting beside a lady minister who was not happy with me jumping up and down. She told me to sit down and she was very cross with me. Well, I just looked at her and burst into tears. I did not cry because she told me off, but because the week before I could not do any of those things. With tears running down my face I said to her "I had a stroke and last week I could not talk, walk or use my hands. No one is going to stop me from praising my God". I believe she felt ashamed. She put her hand on my shoulder and apologised, but the damage was done and I was upset … and that's the truth. I know that it was the enemy trying to stop me from thanking God for His goodness.

At times I still don't remember things, for example I put open milk cartons in cupboards instead of the fridge, or teabags and sugar in the fridge and I'll say to myself "Virg, what are you doing?", but I put it down to my age and laugh my head off. At times I'll be looking everywhere for my glasses only to find that they are on my face! I thank God for giving me a good sense of humour, praise His Holy Name!

Chapter Six

Trust in God

Grateful

Beloved friends, I am just so grateful to Jehovah for healing my body, He is indeed our healer and our deliverer. I am now doing some of the things that He showed me and instructed me to do, Praise His holy name. I can say that I am healed by the stripes of Jesus Christ of Nazareth! The Bible says:

> *Bless the Lord, O my soul; And all that is within me, bless His holy name! Bless the Lord, O my soul, And forget not all His benefits: Who forgives all your iniquities, Who heals all your diseases, Who redeems your life from destruction, Who crowns you with lovingkindness and tender mercies, Who satisfies your mouth with good things, so that your youth is renewed like the eagle's* (Psalm 103:1-5).

Conclusion

I pray that part one of this book will help someone who may be going through similar situations but may not understand why theses things are happening to them. Well, you are not alone. If God healed me, then He will heal you too because He is the same yesterday, today and forever. He heals us and delivers us not because of the things that we do, but according to Lamentations 3:22-23 it is by His grace and mercies which are new every morning. Great is His faithfulness!

Remember Job? He went through great testing. He lost everything that he owned but he never gave up. He trusted God and God came through for him, giving him double of all that he had before. Job received double for his troubles and his latter was greater than his former (see Job chapters 1-3 and 42).

Every one of us has to go through something, whether we are in Christ Jesus or in the world and it is not because God doesn't love us. Sometimes He is trying us to see what is in our heart, or to see whether we will turn our back on Him. The Bible says:

> *Do not think it strange concerning the fiery trial which is to try you, as though some strange thing happened to you* (1 Peter 4:12).

You see, we all have to carry our own cross. He told us to take up our cross and follow Him.

The Word

In the book of Matthew it says:

> *And he who does not take his cross and follow after Me is not worthy of Me* (Matthew 10:38).

> *Now as they came out, they found a man of Cyrene, Simon by name. Him they compelled to bear His cross* (Matthew 27:32).

Jesus Himself had to 'go through'. We will never be able to comprehend what Jesus went through on the cross of Calvary for you and me. He did it just for us so that as we believe in Him, we can become sons and daughters of God:

> *But as many as received Him, to them He gave the right to become children of God, to those who believe in His name* (John 1:12).

Jesus was the ultimate sacrifice for our sins and we will never be able to repay Him for what He has done for us, bless His Holy name! When Jesus was praying in the garden of Gethsemane, He cried out to His Father because of what He was about to go through. The Bible says:

> *He went a little farther and fell on His face, and prayed, saying, "O My Father, if it is possible, let this cup pass from Me; nevertheless, not as I will, but as You will"* (Matthew 26:39).

The Bible goes on to tell us that Jesus understands what we go through:

> *For we do not have a High Priest who cannot sympathize with our weaknesses, but was in all*

points tempted as we are, yet without sin (Hebrews 4:15).

A Prayer

Eternal God, creator of the universe,

We thank you for your goodness and your mercies. Father, I pray that you will bless everyone that reads this book.

Give them a new revelation of the things that concern you. I pray that the God of our Lord Jesus Christ, the Father of glory will give them wisdom, knowledge, understanding and strength to hold on to your unchanging hand.

Continue to lead them into your path of righteousness for your own name's sake. May they be guided by your Spirit and may the favour of God be upon them all. In the name of your Son Jesus the Christ.

Amen.

Part Two: Birth to Salvation

Introduction

Will they revive the stones from the heaps of rubbish, stones that are burned? (Nehemiah 4:2).

After I finished writing part one of this book, which was originally meant to be a separate book in itself, I immediately felt prompted to start writing a second book before the first one was even published. I then felt strongly that the two books should be joined together to form parts one and two of the same book. I felt that in part two I should write about my childhood and about my salvation as I believe that it will help others to understand more about the love that God has for His children.

The confirmation for this came through two of my work colleagues who read the testimonies I shared in part one of how God healed me from some serious illnesses. I knew then that God was speaking.

I would like to give honour to the Father, Son and Holy Spirit for helping me to complete my first book (part one) and for giving me the confidence to start my second one (part two). Praise His holy name!

I started by gathering personal information from my mother and others in my family who knew about my life from the very beginning. My grandmother told me most of what I needed to know about my early years, as I spent most of my childhood with her.

Chapter Seven

My Early Childhood

My Birth

My name is Virginia Douglas (my maiden name is Howe) and I was born in the West Indies on the island of Jamaica. I am the eldest of five children, four girls and one boy. I was told by my mother and other members of my family that my birth was very difficult and that my mother had a hard time bringing me into this world. I was told that after many hours of labour my head was born but my body was left inside the birth canal.

The place where my parents were living at that time had no transportation nearby, so they had to travel on foot or by horse or donkey, which reminds me of the time of Jesus' birth when Mary travelled by donkey!

I was told that they had to carry my mother on a stretcher, just like the ones we use in hospitals today to transfer patients. They had to carry the stretcher to the closest location where the ambulance could come and take mother to hospital and from where a cablegram could be sent to request the ambulance. Under normal circumstances, midwives would visit the homes and deliver the babies, but if there were problems such as this, the patients would be taken to hospital. See Exodus 1:15-19 for more on the role of midwives in Scripture.

One can only imagine how serious this must have been with the head of a baby being born and the body stuck in the womb, but no emergency surgery available. When I look back now I can say that it must have been God. To God be the glory, great things He had done! God kept my mother and I alive. This tells me that satan was after me even before I was born, but God said:

> *Before I formed you in the womb I knew you; Before you were born I sanctified you; I ordained you a prophet to the nations* (Jeremiah 1:5).

I was also told that just before the people who carried the stretcher with my mother got to the main road, one of them slipped on a *stone* and almost dropped the stretcher. All of a sudden the rest of my body came out and I fell to the ground. By this time the ambulance had arrived and they took us to hospital.

At Home

Back in the West Indies, it is very hot and the custom was that during the day people would sit underneath the trees as it was cooler there. My mother said that one day I was asleep under a tree while she did some work outside, then suddenly she heard me scream. She ran to me and saw a large green lizard biting into the left side of my chest. She said that she screamed and grabbed hold of me, causing the lizard to run away.

Mother said that it was a very bad bite and because of that I was sick for a long time; they even thought that I was going to die. Can you imagine the pain I was in? As for mother she must have been very scared but praise the Lord, with the help of God I lived to tell the story.

As a child I remember suffering many things at the hands of 'so-called' family members who led people to believe that they really cared, but the truth is they did not care at all as they treated me badly and did not allow me to go to school.

Mother and Father

Times were hard for mother because even though my father was wealthy in land, cattle, houses and shops, he did not treat mother well. She had to work hard and she suffered many things. My father had many other women and many children. I did not understand it in those days, but now when I look back I realise that their separation came as a result of all of those things.

When they separated, mother had to take me and my sister with her and my brother stayed with our dad. We were the first three children and we were all his. After a while we then went to stay with our grandmother (our mother's mother).

At Age Seven

As the custom was back then, if a family member was wealthy, they would help someone else in the family by taking in one of their children and if they were without children themselves, they would bring up that child as their own.

At about age seven I was sent to stay with one of my father's uncles and his wife. At first they treated me well, but after a while I was just a maidservant doing the same things that the servants did. The woman of the house really did not like me.

One of my jobs was to take care of the pigs and do the housework. Sometimes I would be so hungry that I would eat some of the food I cooked for the pigs, not that the food was bad because they treated their livestock well, but it was the principle of it. It was just like the parable about the prodigal son in Luke 15:11-17, only I did not bring this on myself.

Gran Came to the Rescue

My grandmother must have heard that I was not well cared for because one day she came to visit me unannounced and did not leave without me. That is how I came to live with her, good old gran!

During all of this time mother thought that I was well looked after, but I was not. I believe that out of good manners mother would send messages before she came to visit me, because I always wondered why the lady of the house would suddenly dress me in my Sunday best, sometimes in the middle of the week.

You may ask why I did not tell my mother? I did not tell her because in those days children would not dare to speak or tell tales about adults. If you did, you would get a good 'licking' and no calling 911 (smile).

I was happy at Grandma's. She sent me to school and took good care of me. At school I was loved by the teachers as I was a quiet child and always did as I was told. I did not have to fight with anyone at school because my sister and other children would fight for me back then ... but not now!

Reading and writing was not easy for me but considering the traumatic birth that I had, one would expect something like this. Things were made even more difficult when I did not attend school as often as I should have due to having to take care of my new sisters, but that's just how it was back in those days.

I thought of going back to school when I was older, but I was too embarrassed so I didn't go. The older I got the more embarrassed I got, but glory be to God, later in life when I became a born again Christian, the Holy Spirit helped me and here I am writing this book! Bless His name!

Hard Work

Eventually my mother remarried and went on to have her fourth child, so I had to go and live with her. Being the oldest child I had to work very hard looking after the younger children, doing housework and looking after the animals too as we lived on a farm. Those were hard times for a twelve-year-old.

Attending school became less frequent for me and after two years, along came baby number five, causing the workload to increase even more. My new stepfather loved to beat me whenever the work was not done and although mother didn't like it, she could do nothing about it. By then I almost never attended school.

Beloved friends, I am living proof that hard work never killed anyone and I must add that it taught me to work hard for my living. Even at the age I am now, I am still working hard thanks be to God! Anyway, God created man to work! In the book of Genesis God says:

> *Be fruitful and multiply; fill the earth and subdue it* ... (Genesis 1:28).

In other words, God was saying work the land. The book of Genesis also says that

> *In the sweat of your face you shall eat bread ...* (Genesis 3:19).

So if you want to eat and make a good living, you must work hard and sweat for it!

The good thing is that I was well fed, well cared for and I did not go hungry, unlike when I lived with my uncle.

My mother had a problem with me and my brother because we looked just like our father, so we were a constant reminder to her of our father's behaviour and of the things he put her through. As the saying goes, we were not her 'cup of tea'! Even now after such a long time, whenever she looks at us she always says something negative. He must have hurt her badly.

I would just like to say to anyone who has been hurt by another person, never take it out on your children because it is not their fault. You will damage them mentally and spiritually with your words, because the Bible tells us that:

> *Death and life are in the power of the tongue* (Proverbs 18:21).

Children will grow up to believe the names they are called and they will live out those names. If they constantly hear negative words it will affect them for the rest of their lives, or until they accepted Jesus into their lives and become new creatures, because the Bible says:

> *Therefore, if anyone is in Christ, he is a new creation; old things have passed away; behold, all things have become new* (2 Corinthians 5:17).

Because God created us in His own image, only He knows who we truly are and all that we will become. No human being can ever know us like God knows us because He is Spirit and He made us spirits (see Genesis 1:27-28 and Jeremiah 1:5-9).

When mother remarried she worked even harder than before, but this time the work was different. This time it was in the fields preparing the ground for planting crops such as corn, peas, ginger and different kinds of vegetables. Not only that, but she had to work alongside men where she had to lift heavy loads and carry sugar cane to where the sugar was made and to where the donkeys could be loaded … and guess who was working right alongside mother, me!

Beloved friends, this is not just a story, this is the truth. Only people who were born in the West Indies in those days will be able to fully understand what I am saying. Those were hard times, praise God!

After some years my stepfather got himself another woman, so he and my mother separated. He took his two girls to his father's house and mother packed and went off to stay with my grandmother, taking me and my other sister who was also my father's child. All three of us stayed with good old gran for a while. After some time mother went to look for work in the town area. She started to work as a shopkeeper as well as doing housework, until eventually she managed to get rented accommodation.

After a while I went to live with her and my second sister went to stay with relatives, visiting only on weekends. Mother worked hard and was eventually able to get a bigger place, so then my other two sisters started to visit on weekends. I must say that mother was very honest, so everywhere she worked they loved her and she always had favour with the people she worked for, so did all of us.

One particular family she worked for was from the Czech Republic. Mother was nanny to their two girls and they treated us like their own family. Even now after so many years, one of those girls stills looks after mother's affairs as my sister and I are unable to because we live abroad. This lady is now playing the role of a daughter to my mother and we all accepted her as our sister. Because of her status, she married a wealthy man and is now one of the wealthiest women in our hometown.

Chapter Eight

My Teenage Years

Back to Me

By the time I was fourteen-years-old it was time for me start working, so I got a job as a nanny looking after a child by the name of Len. My main duties were to bathe and feed him, take him out for walks in his pram, do his laundry and so on … you know, the basic nanny duties. I got on well with the family and they treated well which was good because not everybody treated you well as a worker.

Now when I look back, I realise that God had a plan for my life because of His grace, His mercies, His love and His favour. The Bible says:

> *Through the Lord's mercies we are not consumed, Because His compassions fail not. They are new every morning; Great is Your faithfulness* (Lamentations 3:22-23).

That is why I agree with the songwriter who wrote, *'When I think of the goodness of Jesus and what He has done for me, my soul cries out hallelujah, thank God for saving me*'.

My Own Child

I was fifteen-years-old by then and as I took Len for walks morning and evening, I became friends with a boy of my own age. In those days I was very naive, even at fifteen-years-old. I did not know that one could become pregnant so easily, I just listened to my older friends and fell into the trap! Just to show how naive I was, my belly began to grow but I just thought that I was eating too much, not knowing that I was eating for two (smile).

It's funny though how this pregnancy happened, because my mother always had a chaperone with me when I was not at my job. What can I say? Chaperones have to sleep sometime don't they … and where there is a will, there is a way!

So one day I said to mother, "What are you putting in your cooking? I seem to be getting fatter every day". She looked at me in amazement and said, "I am taking you to the doctor", so she did. When the doctor announced the news, she looked at me with such a bad look that I thought to myself I am done for now ... she is going to kill me for making her a grandmother at such a young age. I tell you, she did not spank me but she called me every name under the sun, you know what I mean? Anyway, it did not take too long for her to calm down.

Eventually the time came and the baby was born. Mother took complete control. The way it was back then is that the grandmother would be the one to take charge of looking after any new baby, or if she was not around then a near relative or friend would do that job. The mother of the child would just do the feeding until three months were up then she would be able to do a little more for the baby.

It was not hard for me to look after the baby because I'd had a lot of practise with my younger sisters and as I said before, I was a nanny as well. The baby was a boy weighing four-and-a-half pounds at birth, but he soon began to grow. Now my son is 5ft 6ins tall whereas I am only 4ft 10ins!

Chapter Nine

A Mother of Two

Another Move

When my baby was one-year-old, an opportunity came for mother to travel to England. One of her aunt's daughters was living in England at the time and helped her to come over. It was a great opportunity because in those days many people were coming to England for work.

Mother did well in her job and at the time she stayed with her cousin so she did not have to pay rent. She was able to save money so that she could eventually send for us and she would always send us nice clothes, amongst other things.

After a while she was able to get her own apartment and at some point along the way she found herself a new husband. I was over the moon because the gentleman's name was the same as the name of the child that I was a nanny to. This gentleman treated mother very well.

A Big Chance

Mother was very happy with her new husband and her fine lifestyle, he bought mother her first house. Can you imagine? When the news reached us we were so happy!

The news spread like wildfire and boy, when she came to visit us all those who didn't care about her before when she was struggling didn't know what to do with themselves. Now they had to respect her and even ask her for help. My grandmother used to say to mother when she was in her struggles and people were making fun of her, "Wha-no-dead-no-tek–it-dash-wey", or in proper English, "If it is not dead, do not throw it away!".

The first visit mother made home was to help make preparations to send for us to come to England ... and may I add that it was her husband's idea. How wonderful was that?

I would have been the first one to travel, but sadly I was pregnant again at that time with my second child, my daughter. There was a falling out between me and my son's father and we were not married. It just so happened that he moved to another town to work and in the process, he found another girl and had another child. He was just like my father, he too had a lot of women! Word eventually got to me about it and so I ended the relationship with him. It was at this time that I met my daughter's father.

As I could not travel to England at that time my second sister went instead, then after the birth of my daughter I was able to come over. My daughter was just two-years-old at the time.

I had to leave my son with his grandmother, then when I came over and got settled I sent for him to come and join us.

Chapter Ten

A New Life in England

My Arrival

I arrived in England in the month of November, so it was very cold and it was snowing. My original flight had been cancelled and I ended up arriving on a different day, but by the time I arrived it was too late to contact mother so no one came to meet me. What an experience I had! It is a good thing that I had a letter with me that had mother's address on it. I asked one of the airport workers if he knew where the place was and he said no, but he got me a black cab. This was in the early sixties and it was much safer back then.

Well, me and my daughter who was just two-years-old at the time were not dressed for the British weather! The cab driver had to turn the heater right up so that we could be warm, bless him. We made our way from the airport to Islington in London.

I looked through the window of the cab as we travelled but I could hardly see a thing. "Very strange," I said to the driver, "me can't-see-a-ting!". This is what we call Jamaican patois. He laughed and said, "What did you say?", so I repeated it, "can't-see-nu-ting". He laughed again and said, "Oh, you cannot see anything!", I said, "Yes". He said, "It is fog". It was funny, I couldn't understand him very well and he couldn't understand me either, well what do you expect, I had just come off the plane! Thank God it wasn't a boat (smile).

As we travelled the fog lifted and I could see more clearly. The buildings looked strange. I asked the driver "Why do they have so many prisons over here?", pointing to some building. He laughed and said they were houses. I had never seen houses like those. You must understand that at home, houses were no higher than two stories, or small bungalow type houses, or little houses made of wood with grass roofs (not mud huts I might add); I am talking about the West Indies. They were similar to what the Americans call cabins.

We finally arrived in Islington and parked outside this huge house which looked like a prison. The driver got out of the cab, banged on the large door then came back to get me. Well, I refused point blank to get out of the cab, I told the driver to take me back to the airport! He started to laugh again, then I saw a white lady open the door. The driver spoke to her and asked if there was a lady by the name of Mrs Dunn living there and she said yes (this was my mother's married name).

The lady said to the driver "I am going to get my coat", but in my mind she was going for the police because remember, to me this place was like a prison (smile). However she came back out with her coat on and told us her name. She said my mother was at work, then she paid the driver and took us into the house. She made a phone call to where mother worked to let her know that we had arrived and I felt better then. The lady was happy to see us and fell in love with the baby, mind you my daughter was very pretty and could easily have passed for a white child as her father was very fair/light-skinned. Anyway, she fed the baby milk and fed me fish and chips.

When mother came home she was so happy that she didn't know what to do with herself! She started to prepare a celebration meal and by then, my sister and her husband had come home from work with two of their children. The celebration started, then later my mother's husband came home. He was lovely! There was a lot of jumping and dancing going on and when I told them what I had said to the cab driver everyone laughed. It was so good to be with my family after such a long time.

Now when my daughter and I arrived, the lady who came out to meet us took an instant liking to my daughter and I don't know why, but I could see that my daughter liked her as well. When my mother tried to pick my daughter up she ran to the other lady and would not let mother hold her. Mother did not like that at all, but after a while my daughter started to follow mother around calling her 'nana'. She used to call my grandmother the same name back in Jamaica.

Anyway, guess what, the house I thought was a prison turned out to be my mother's first house, all fourteen rooms ... in one house! She had rented out some of the rooms and the family lived in the rest. Each person had their own flat but the tenants shared a kitchen and bathroom.

Well, I could see that my mother's life had turned around for the better. She had gone from working in remote places and working as a servant living in rented accommodation, to becoming a landlord, praise be to

God! God's ways are past finding out. In the book of Isaiah God tells us that His thoughts are not our thoughts and neither are His ways our ways (Isaiah 55:8).

Working in a New Land

I had a few weeks to get used to the cold weather before I started working. The company that mother worked for had sent me a work permit before I came over. This is how I got a job working at the same company as my mother. So, my first job in England was making umbrellas. It was fun and the people who worked there called me Millie Small after a famous young Jamaican singer who sang a song called 'My Boy Lollipop'.

I was happy in my new job. It was very different from being a nanny but it was a good experience. By then my daughter had started nursery school and I would pick her up after work. Sometimes it would be so dark and foggy that I could hardly see where I was going. Sometimes it would be snowing and very cold. At those times I felt that I wanted to go back home, but I persevered and when summer came I soon changed my mind.

The company we worked for eventually closed down and we were made redundant, but after a while we all got other jobs. It was easy to get jobs in those days, you could walk out of a job in the morning and get another the same day.

I got a job just ten minutes walk from home doing soldering and making cufflinks, belts and shoe buckles. This kind of work was called 'piecework'. Piecework meant that you only got paid for the amount of work that you did, so if you wanted to earn more money you had to work hard for it, which I did ... no doubt about that! It was fun in those days and we always seemed to work for good managers who treated us fairly. If you were a good worker you would get promoted easily.

After some time this company also closed down and again I was made redundant, but I soon got yet another job. At that time I was still living at mother's house and so I was able to save money each week, which was good because I was able to send money and clothes home for my son who was still living with his grandmother in Jamaica. I even started to talk about helping my daughter's father to come to England. He was living in Nassau at the time and we kept in touch, but mother said no. Let me explain, mother was always in control and I always had to do what she said whether I liked it or not, so if she said no, it was no!

Mother Had a Plan

Mother said that as she did not know my daughter's father, it would be better if I married my son's father because he had stood by me when I had my son and because she liked him. I explained to her that he was just like my father when it came to women. I told her that he was living with someone else and that he'd had a child with this other woman before I came to England, but she would not hear of it.

We did not speak about the matter again for a long time after that so I thought she had forgotten about it, but I was wrong. One day out of the blue, she told me that she had paid the air fare for my son's father to come over and that she had also gotten him a job. Then she told me his arrival date and explained that he was coming because we were to be married. Boy, you could have knocked me over with a feather, can you imagine how upset I was?

I could not argue with her out of respect, so I give in to her plan. All the wedding arrangements were made by her. When he arrived (I'll call him 'Mr'), he seemed to have calmed down a lot. He told me that he was a changed person and that he wouldn't let me down. Deep down I did not believe him but I decided to give him the benefit of the doubt. Boy was I right to have my doubts! How can a leopard change its spots? It was not long before the same thing started all over again … his womanising that is.

Chapter Eleven

Married Life

The Wedding

The wedding day finally came and we were married, but at the reception he was so busy with the girls that some other fellow had to carry me over the threshold. How can that be right? It was wrong for that to take place, but mother just clapped and laughed. I didn't know any better until it was too late.

My daughter's father and I had always discussed marriage in our letters to each other. He always said that he would never marry anyone else unless I married someone first, so I had to write to him and give him the news. As you can imagine he was very upset about the whole matter, but there was nothing either of us could do. From time to time I would write to let him know how his daughter was, but my new husband said that I should stop because he would now take care of us. So I did as I was told. Mother agreed with him, so to keep the peace I stopped writing and lost contact.

I kept all the letters and a couple of photographs because I wanted my daughter to know what her father looked like, even if it was just a picture. I had planned that I would show her his letters when she was the right age, however one day 'Mr' found the photos and some of the letters and destroyed them even though I told him the reason for keeping them. Anyway, I had some other letters which he did not find.

When my daughter was about twelve-years-old she asked me where the photographs of her dad were. I told her that her new dad had thrown them away, but I showed her the remaining letters that I had. We read them and laughed together.

Moving House

The time came for us to move house as my son was now with us and we needed a bigger place. We applied for a house in outer London and we were granted a three bedroom house, so we moved out of mother's house which was a good thing. At least mother was not going to be there to give orders.

Things went well for a while. The children were happy in their new school and 'Mr' and I started our new jobs. He worked for London Transport and I got a job in a hospital as a care nurse, but it wasn't long before he was up to his old tricks again running around with other women. This time it was more than one woman and he had the audacity to tell one of them that he was living with his sister rather than saying that I was his wife, can you believe that? Things between us began to get a little intense. At times he would deny it, even when he'd been caught … beloved friends I am telling the truth!

As soon as I would leave for work he would bring someone into the house, even my own friends sometimes. As we both did shift work, this gave him more opportunities to do what he wanted when he wanted. He even had the cheek to tell me that my friends were his friends as well. To tell you the truth, sometimes I had to laugh because it was just so unbelievable.

Well, I stayed in the marriage for twelve years, but it got to the stage where I'd had enough, so one day I spoke to him about the situation. I told him that if he didn't change his ways I would end the marriage, but he just laughed at me saying that I didn't know what I was saying. Of course at that time I was not yet born again (saved). I mentioned it to my mother but she just told me that he would change, clearly she had forgotten what had happened between her and my father.

Proof

Eventually I found proof of what was going on and I decided I was going to do something about it. I spoke to him again but he still would not stop. Maybe he thought that he was like King Solomon in the Bible, "*But King Solomon loved many foreign women ...*" (1 Kings 11:1).

I found a lawyer and started proceedings. When the papers arrived he called my mother and told her, but she told him that I could never do that, that I was not serious and that he should pay no attention to it. Well, he signed the papers and returned them to me and I stuck to my guns, I did not change my mind. Things took a few months to come through, but when he eventually received the court date he could not believe it. He was mad at me and claimed that I only ever did what other people told me to do and that I would change my mind ... but I didn't.

After a while he moved in with the younger of the two ladies he was seeing and they had three children together. You may find this strange but despite everything that happened, we still remain friends up until this day. Anyway, the new girl became friends with my daughter as they were close in age and we were all like one big happy family. People told me that I was stupid but I ignored them and guess what, it paid off for me in the end!

What Goes Around ...

It did not take long for 'Mr' to do the same thing to the young lady that he did to me. He went and married my best friend whilst still living with this girl and their children. When she found out, he denied it saying that the woman had married him by deed poll and that he didn't know about it. This is a true story, I am not making this up ... believe me!

The poor girl was devastated! She called me because she didn't know what to do and I ended up being the only shoulder she had to cry on in her time of need. I could easily have made fun of her but I didn't, I stepped in and helped her like an elder sister instead. I did not know it at the time, but God was training me and teaching me how to love my neighbour, even though I was not yet born again.

After some years I got sick, by which time my daughter had four children of her own and moved to America, but this same young woman stepped in and helped as though she was my own daughter. Even after I got better she was there still helping me out. When I moved house she came with her sister and decorated my flat, so I ended up not having to pay anyone to do the decorating. This had to be God! Bless His holy name!

Beloved friends, the good that you do for others will continue to live on after you. I often wonder what would have happened if I had turned my back on this girl in her time of need. Remember, this is the same girl that was with my ex-husband while we were still married, can you believe it? The good thing is that we still remain friends to this day and I can call her at any time. Sometimes when we meet we talk about the past and laugh at the whole matter, because 'Mr' used to tell her that I was his sister ... but look at God!

'Mr' Retired

Eventually 'Mr' retired from London Transport and went back home. He built a mansion back in the West Indies and left England with his new wife, the one who he said married him by deed poll! Well, if that's not laughable what is? But sadly, the other girl was left behind with her three children.

My son is now a grown man but even he doesn't know what to make of it all, however he still keeps in touch with 'Mr', which is not a bad thing. I have forgiven him because the Lord would not have it any other way.

Chapter Twelve

God Had a Plan

What I am about to share in the next two chapters is a very serious matter. I pray that the things I experienced will help others, but my main reason for sharing it is to prove just how awesome our God is and how defeated satan is.

These incidents took place before I became born again, which brings me to the text in Jeremiah which reads:

> *Before I formed you in the womb I knew you; Before you were born I sanctified you; I ordained you a prophet to the nations* (Jeremiah 1:5).

Amen! The story goes like this.

About three years after my marriage ended, I was working in a hospital and basically just getting on with my life. I was not looking for another relationship at that time and I would say to myself, "I will never go through what I've being through again". Since becoming a Christian I now realise that those words were curses.

A New Relationship

Anyway, one day a very handsome man approached me and asked me out. I did not say yes straightaway, but after a while I agreed. This person was someone who worked in the medical field, or should I say used to be in that field.

My work colleagues would say that I was lucky (blessed) and at the time to tell you the truth, I thought so too. The Bible tells us about an angel of light not always being what he appears to be (see 2 Corinthians 11:14), but I did not know the Bible at that time, until it was almost too late … but God!

My relationship with this handsome man started well. I was happy and he treated me like a queen. I wore the best clothes, ate the best food, went on lots of holidays and I must say, I enjoyed it all! But little did I know what lay ahead! All of my family liked him and I took him to the West Indies to meet mother, who by then had moved back home to Jamaica and she too liked him very much.

After being together for two years he moved in with me and it was great, he did almost everything for me. At times when I came home from work even my bath was ready and my dinner waiting in the oven, it was great! We lived together for five years, but after a while I noticed that he was becoming more and more protective of me. It got so bad that he would even stand outside the bathroom door whenever I was in there. When I asked him why, he would say that someone could come in and hurt me so he had to protect me.

Over time, it got worse and worse and I just couldn't understand it. He would even phone my workplace and tell them that I was sick when I was not. It got to the point where he would not even go to work because in his mind he thought that I would be killed.

My goodness, it became very scary and it was happening on and off for about a year. I did not know what to do. I tried to get him to see a doctor but he would not go, he always said that he was fine. I even talked to his parents, but they told me not to worry and that he would be fine because it was something that happened sometimes, but it would pass. Even though they reassured me, I was still worried and it became clear that they had lied because the situation got worse.

It was funny, most of the time things were fine, when he was not being overprotective that is. But then one day he told me that he was going to take me to a place that he visited from time to time; there was something very strange about the way he said it. He ordered a four poster bed, I cannot say where from, but it was large and beautiful. He also ordered two large fans which I believe were from one of the eastern countries. I have never seen anything like it before or since. One of the fans was large enough to cover one whole side of the bed, like a curtain ... and then the other one covered the other side of the bed.

I was living in a block of flats at the time, so when the bed arrived it came in parts on a truck and the delivery men assembled it inside the flat. My neighbours were wondering what on earth was going on, so when the bed was assembled they all came in to see it and they started to call me 'Queen Victoria'. Praise God!

What Happened Next

Beloved friends, let me give you an analogy so as not to scare you too much when you read what happened next.

Back in the West Indies, about six months before Christmas a pig or a couple of chickens would be fed very well in order to be fattened up for Christmas dinner. Right up until the night before Christmas, that pig and those chickens would enjoy their food and if they could talk, they would probably say to one another "We are special!", not knowing that the next day they would be on the dinner table, not as a guest but as the food … you may laugh but it is the truth.

During the next seven years several attempts were made on my life. It is only now that I realise that it was the angels of God who were protecting me from the onslaught of satan. When all of those things were happening I was not yet born again, but God had a plan for my life.

You may ask why I did not leave, but how can a bird fly away when the cage is locked? Well, I can tell you how the cage eventually became unlocked, it was unlocked by the King of Kings! Beloved friends, I am living proof that God is no respecter of persons and that He will never leave us or forsake us. I know that this may sound a little far-fetched to some of you, but I am a child of God and this is a testimony of God's grace and His mercies even to the unsaved, because the Bible says that the sun shines on the just and on the unjust (see Matthew 5:45). Amen.

Now it fell on a day in the month of July in the 1990s, a day that I will never forget, that I came home from work as usual to find that dinner was ready and my bath was ready, but there was a sense of fear about this person. He looked sad, as a matter of fact he was crying. I asked him what was wrong but he just looked at me and shook his head.

I had my bath and when I came out dinner was on the table. I ate, then as usual I went to sit in the living room. He came and sat beside me and held my hands, but then I saw something that made me afraid. His face changed and as he spoke, his voice changed and sounded like many voices, it was like being in a horror movie. I couldn't believe my eyes and I began to shake at what the voices were saying to me.

Then in the twinkling of an eye he changed back to normal. He looked at me and asked why I looked so frightened. I asked him whether he knew what had just happened and he said no, so I told him what I had just seen and heard. He said that he would never hurt me but that sometimes you have to give up the one that you love. I then pretended that I needed to go to the bathroom which was near the front door, but when I looked, all three locks on the door were locked, can you imagine the state I was in?

I then heard a voice behind me saying, "You cannot get out, today is the day". When I looked back I saw that his face had changed back to the same face of horror again. Then he suddenly started to look at me as though he was actually seeing people that he hated and he began to call me by their names. He said to me "Look in the bedroom" and when I looked, I saw for the first time all of the preparations that had been made. When I saw it, all I could say was "Lard-me-Gad, help me!", or in English, "Lord my God, help me!". I cannot explain to you what I saw ... all I can say is that only God knows!

The Rescue

I was rescued from this situation just in time, because we serve an on time God! You see, the plan was that there was supposed to be an exchange of power for a life and not just any life, but the life of someone he loved. Satan does not care about people's lives. Because we are made in the image of God satan's plan is to steal, kill and destroy, but God's plan is that we might have life and have it more abundantly:

> *The thief does not come except to steal, and to kill, and to destroy. I have come that they may have life, and that they may have it more abundantly* (John 10:10).

After being together for seven years, the time came when satan tried to use this man to destroy what God had made. Sometimes people will sell their own soul to the devil to gain things in life, whether it be money or so-called power, but in my case it was both. The devil will always try to use people to do his dirty work, but praise God ... I lived to tell the tale!

Beloved friends, it would not be wise for me to go into detail about exactly how this life-changing situation took place, but just remember the analogy I gave about the Christmas chicken and pig! The main thing is that even though all of this took place before I became a Christian, God still sent His angels to deliver me! The Bible says:

> *For He shall give His angels charge over you, To keep you in all your ways* (Psalm 91:11).

Our God is an awesome God … He is worthy to be praised! God has created us in His own image and He has created us for a purpose. His will must be done in our lives, which is one of the reasons why I have such a passion for the things of God. If it was not for the Lord who was on my side, I would not be living today to tell of my ordeal. Praise be to God!

Beloved friends, I had almost seven years of happiness in that relationship, or so I thought, but it soon turned to sorrow. As the Bible says, when we think there is peace, sudden destruction comes (see 1 Thessalonians. 5:3). The Bible also says:

> *Weeping may endure for a night, but joy comes in the morning* (Psalm 30:5).

Well, I soon realised that there was a war going on in that house and I was very scared. It was as though this one man was fighting with an invisible army and as he fought, he was saying, "I will not open the door, this is the day!". It looked to me as though someone unseen was pushing him towards the door. After a long time he finally he gave in and unlocked the door, cursing and shouting at me to get my demons off him.

Before I go any further let me say this, it is only since I became born again that I realise that this person was fighting with the angels of God. Even though I was not yet saved God still sent His angels to protect me! The Bible says:

> *The angel of the Lord encamps all around those who fear Him, And delivers them* (Psalm 34:7).

And yes I did fear the Lord! The Bible goes on to say:

> *Many are the afflictions of the righteous, But the Lord delivers him out of them all* (Psalm 34:19).

When God released those locks on the door and opened it, I ran for my life! I went to the house of a friend who lived about fifteen minutes walk from the flat and who was a Christian.

When I got there I was out of breath with fear written all over my face. Immediately my friend began to pray warfare prayers. I have now come to understand why she prayed that way. As I listened to her pray I became even more scared, but eventually her prayer calmed me down and I was able to tell her what happened. She knew about the problem from when it started, but she did not know that it had gone so far, so I told her about all the events in detail.

That night I stayed at my friend's house and I remembered that she would always tell me about Jesus and that I should give my life to Him. I always told her that I was not ready, however after the events of that day I was prepared to do anything, not just for myself but also to help this man. Why you may ask? Because he was good to me and he treated me like a queen for seven years.

I did not say yes to my friend's invitation to accept Christ on the same day, but not long after that I accepted Jesus as my Lord and Savour. From that day, I have not looked back and I found out that it was the best decision I ever made. I sometimes ask myself why I waited so long to make the decision, but as I began to grow in God, I knew why. The Bible says:

> *So I sought for a man among them who would make a wall, and stand in the gap before Me on behalf of the land, that I should not destroy it; but I found no one* (Ezekiel 22:30).

I was one of those that God was looking for and that is why the enemy tried to stop me ... but if God is for us, who can be against us (see Romans 8:38). Praise God!

Anyway, the flat I had shared with this man was actually rented accommodation in my name, so with the help of the law he was removed and I then went back, but it was very scary.

After That

He started to make threatening phone calls which kept coming in the middle of the night, so much so that I could not sleep, but worst of all the flat felt like there was black darkness over it. Evil was all around and unusual things were happening which I could not explain. I could not stay another night in that place so I packed my clothes and went to stay with my daughter. I gave up the flat and left what I call the 'evil bed' and applied for another place.

One day not long after that, I spotted him near my house and had to run and hide, I was so frightened. He was calling out to me saying, "I won't hurt you, I just want to talk", well I ran even faster! I had not been born again for long so I was very fearful and there was no way that I would go anywhere near him. Can you imagine how it felt to run away from someone I had known so well ... or thought I knew!

Chapter Thirteen

Accepting Christ: My Call to Ministry

As time went on, I began to grow in the things of God and became stronger in my faith. I knew this because the next time I saw him I was less fearful. I was able to speak with him and even prayed for him … with caution you understand, I would pray with my eyes open! Over time as I continued to grow, I found that I was no longer afraid. After a while I no longer saw him and I was told that this was because he was in a hospital. I will be honest and say that I felt safer on the road after hearing that, but I still continued to pray for him, praise God.

As I grew stronger in the things of God, I began to enjoy praying for people and God connected me and a friend together as prayer partners. The church we attended was serious about spiritual warfare, so I was quickly trained in that area. I believe that I was born to be a prayer warrior because the Lord Himself began to teach me spiritual warfare, bless His name.

Training for Ministry

I began to do some training in the areas that I believed God had called me into, which were three areas: intercession, prayer counselling and the deliverance ministry. How do I know this? Because from the moment

I became born again these were the areas that I was most excited to learn about. As a matter of fact, even before I was saved I had been counselling people who had experienced a stillbirth, because I'd had the same experience.

As I was working in hospitals where many painful things happened, it seemed that I was always supporting others who were in distress. So this was not only at church, because it seemed that everywhere I went there would be someone in need of comfort in one way or another. I was pleased when I found this Scripture in the Word of God:

> *"Comfort, yes, comfort My people!" Says your God* (Isaiah 40:1).

I grew even stronger in the Lord and in His word. Visiting ministers would speak over my life and confirm the Word of God that was over my life, so I continued to do what God said in His word.

The Bible says:

> *Be diligent to present yourself approved to God, a worker who does not need to be ashamed, rightly dividing the word of truth* (2 Timothy 2:15).

I started to attend teaching sessions to learn more about the physical side of the areas of ministry I believe I am called to, then God took over and taught me about the spiritual side. How did He do that? By His word and in dreams and visions. Believe me, God literally teaches me things, especially in spiritual warfare. He trained me like one would train a soldier. Maybe that's why I am the way that I am, what do I mean? I behave like a soldier, I act crazy in warfare.

There was no doubt in my mind about the areas of ministry that I was called into because it was clearly seen by others and confirmed by God. I must stress that the training was not easy, it came with troubles, pain, sickness and serious attacks from the enemy which I am still experiencing right up to this day! But praise God, I made up my mind to stay in the fight. Paul said that we should "*Fight the good fight of faith, lay hold on eternal life*" (1 Timothy 6:12) and as we know, the battle belongs to God.

God Himself revealed to me the areas of ministry that He has called me to and He gave me the gifts to operate in them, so I do it with passion. I am not saying that I have not made mistakes along the way because I know that I am not perfect, but it is only because of His grace and His mercies that I am able to do it. One songwriter said, "*It's a hard road to travel and a mighty long way to go*", so I am still pressing on the upward way, or as the Apostle Paul says, I press toward the mark of the high calling of God (see Philippians 3:14).

The Lord has been calling me since I was quite young, but I did not want to leave my sinful life. I was busy enjoying myself, or so I thought. When others would tell me about giving my life to the Lord, my response was always that I was not ready ... until that awful day when I nearly lost my life. But as the Bible says:

> *There is a way that seems right to a man, But its end is the way of death* (Proverbs 16:25).

God has to bring some of us to the point of death before we come to our senses and recognise that what the Bible says is true, "… *the wages of sin is death, but the gift of God is eternal life …*" (Romans 6:23), bless His name! God does not put pressure on us to do anything, He gives us a free will, but He said:

> *Behold, I stand at the door and knock. If anyone hears My voice and opens the door, I will come in to him and dine with him, and he with Me* (Revelation 3:20).

God will allow some things to come our way so that we may know that He is the way, the truth and the life and that we cannot go to the Father but through Him (see John 14:6).

God has brought me from a mighty long way and as He says in Jeremiah 1:5, He knew me before He formed me in my mother's womb. With all the things that I have been through, I know of a surety that it is God that has brought me through. He says in His word:

> *When you pass through the waters, I will be with you; And through the rivers, they shall not overflow you. When you walk through the fire, you shall not be burned, Nor shall the flame scorch you.* (Isaiah 43:2).

He also says:

> *I know the thoughts that I think toward you, says the Lord, thoughts of peace and not of evil, to give you a future and a hope* (Jeremiah 29:11).

I am still walking in the way of the Lord and enjoying His presence, though He still has to reprove me at times to remind me that it is "… *'not by might nor by power, but by My Spirit,' Says the Lord of hosts*" (Zechariah 4:6).

In Conclusion

I pray that this book will help someone who may be going through similar situations to know that they can do all things through Christ who strengthens us (see Philippians 4:13) and that all we have to do is trust in Him, why? Because He is GOD! The Bible does not tell us that this Christian walk will be easy, but it tells us:

> *For whom the Lord loves He chastens, And scourges every son whom He receives* (Hebrews 12:6).

I pray that the blessings of God the Father, God the Son and God the Holy Ghost will rest upon all who read this book. God bless you all. Amen.

* 9 7 8 1 7 8 4 5 6 3 0 2 8 *

ND - #0190 - 060826 - C0 - 216/138/9 - PB - 9781784563028 - Gloss Lamination